Philippi's Crawley

An Immigrant's Dream

Of a Model Village

Ian T Henderson

Philippi's Crawley
First printed in Great Britain by
C M Printing Services
20a Jewry Street
Winchester
Copyright © 1977 Ian T Henderson

New edition published by
Leopard Publishing Ventures Ltd
Hampshire SO212PR
www.thehalfdays.com
www.magickgate.com

A CIP catalogue record is available from the British Library.

ISBN: 9780995708518

Contents

Contents

Foreword

My father Ian Henderson arrived in Crawley in 1962 quite by chance. He had sold his house in Chawton and was looking for a new village house form which he could commute to the City. Upon wandering to the Fox and Hounds, he was greeted by: "Henderson, what are you doing here?" from Colin Conte, the landlord. Colin and my father had been fellow groomsmen at a wedding in Cairo during the Second World War.

Colin had promised to keep an eye out for a suitable abode, and when the Gribbons decided to sell Pond House, he immediately phoned my father, who left a board meeting and travelled straight down by train to see it. As was typical of him, he offered them the asking price straight away and they shook hands. A local estate agent then phoned to offer a further viewing to which Mrs. Gribbon replied: "I am sorry but we have sold it!"

Having married my father 10 weeks earlier after meeting on the liner back from New York, my mother Imelda arrived in Crawley 18 months later. She had been a theatre actress for most of her life from a large theatrical family in Belfast. Local friends in Crawley all rallied round as she successfully transitioned from a life on the boards to life in a most English village. Judging from the family photos, I believe they must have had a lot of fun.

My father sadly died not long after the publication of this original book. He had been in stockbroking and business leadership most of his life. His real passion, however, was for books and publishing. Just as I am doing now, he ran his publishing business out of Pond House, producing historical volumes on Golf, Pictorial China and, of course, *The Winchester Diver*. His interest in Ernest Philippi was not only as the local landlord who did much to shape the character of the village of Crawley, but also as a captain of industry who transformed the Glasgow cotton industry in the late nineteenth and early twentieth century. The concept of leadership and the inspiration of business leaders was an ideal close to his heart. I know he would have been pleased to see this short, but poignant volume on Philippi's Crawley revisited.

My mother sadly passed away recently after a period of ill health, although still able to sing beautifully right up until the very end. She was delighted to see an early proof of the new version of this book. In an ironic twist, she was of course another great example of a successful immigrant who has flourished in Crawley.

I cannot thank them both enough for such a wonderful upbringing here and all that they have done for me. This book is a small token of thanks to them and the wonderful village and people of Crawley who have always been so very kind.

I would like to thank my co-conspirator, business partner and editor of this revised publication, Sedley Proctor. With a keen eye and a very thoughtful approach, he has cleverly updated it and kept the charm of the original work.

Thank you also to Michelle Price for kind permission to use her late mother's drawings again, and although Coral Northeast is no longer resident in Crawley, I trust that she will be happy for us to continue to publish her late father's drawings as well.

Tony Henderson
In Loco Parentis, September 2018

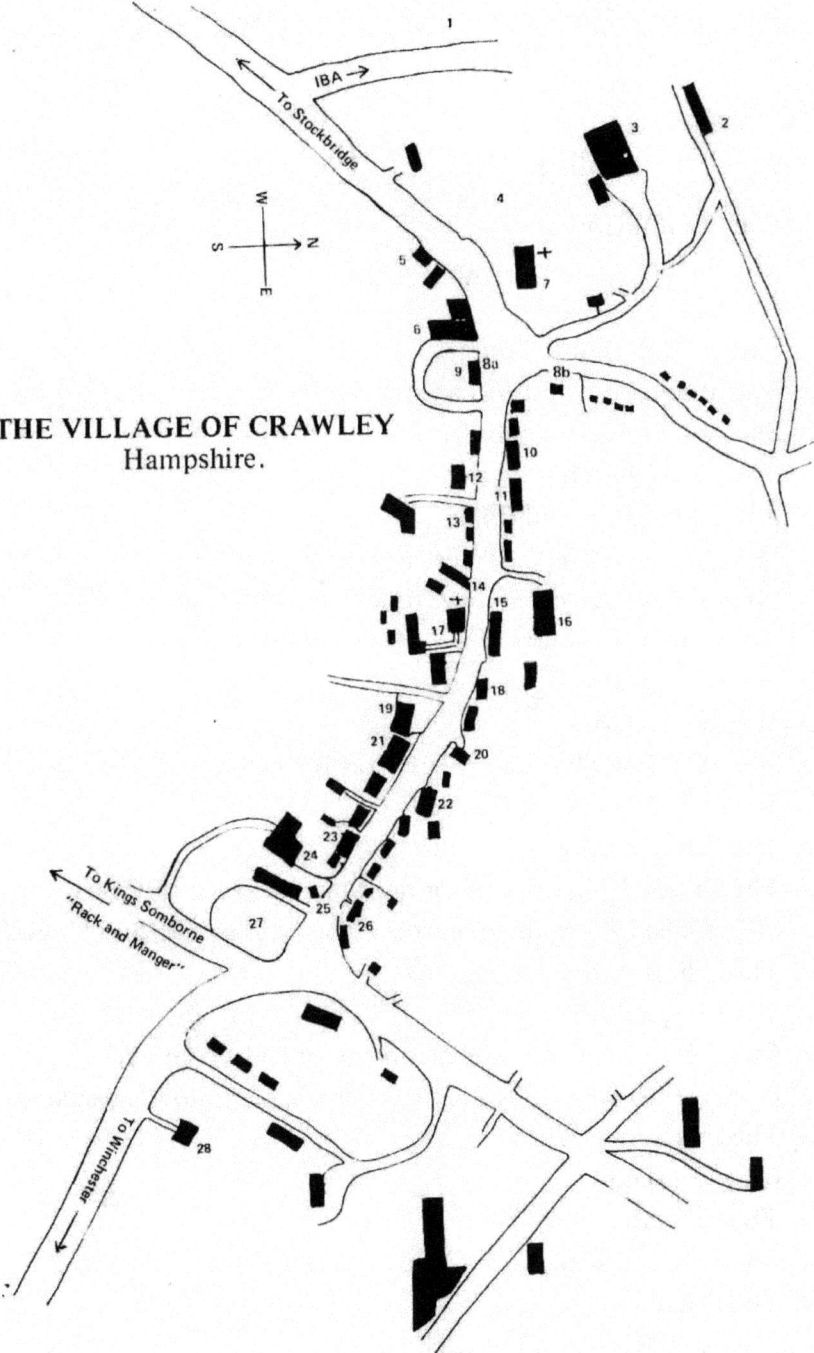

THE VILLAGE OF CRAWLEY
Hampshire.

Map of Village of Crawley

1977

Village Directory 1900-1930

1. Site of Golf Course
2. The Stables – Crawley Court
3. Site of Crawley Court
4. Site of Real Tennis Court
5. Site of Squash Court (now Chalk Hills)
6. Site of Old Rectory (now The Dower House)
7. St Mary's Church
8. Site of Forge (a) and (b)
9. Pear Tree Cottage (gas lamp and Insurance sign)
10. Original site of Post Office (now Glenbuck Cottage)
11. Later site of Post Office and Bakery (now 4 residencies)
12. Site of second village pond
13. Site of Laundry
14. Site of Village Shop (now The Coach House)
15. Site of Village Domestic Well
16. The White House
17. The Village Hall, site of Skating Rink and Bowling Green
18. Site of The Jolly Sportsman (now The Homestead) and Horse Ties
19. The Village School
20. The Gospel Hall
21. Oak Cottages (Tudor Style) and site of Village Green
22. Orchard Cottages (Bavarian style conversion: now 2 residences)
23. The Fox and Hounds
24. Crawley Manor
25. The Fire House
26. Pond House (with Farm Office and Bath House in garage)
27. The Pond
28. The New Rectory (now Glebe House)

ACKNOWLEDGMENTS

Curiosity regarding Ernest Philippi took me to Glasgow to see Mr. C J Risk, the Secretary of Coats Patons Ltd, who had already shown interest and enthusiasm for the story of this great industrialist. I am grateful to him for providing the research material on which part of this story is based and for permission to inspect the J & P Coats' archives. I would like to thank all those who live in the neighbourhood who have been helpful in providing memories of life in Crawley or at the Court at the time. I would also like to thank Mrs. Georgina Rose, granddaughter of Ernest Philippi, for her help and for the loan of diaries, photographs, etc. Finally, I am particularly indebted to Mrs. Patricia Asa Thomas for being responsible for the illustrations which include her own drawings and to Mrs. Patricia Rawson for her preparation of the script.

Ian T Henderson

March 1977

View of Village Street across the Pond: on the left, The Fire House, on the right, Pond House

The Village of Crawley

Hampshire

The extensive Downs of Central Hampshire are bounded, on the west, by the River Test and, on the south, by the River Itchen. Alongside these rivers and their tributaries there are numerous villages, but on the Central Downs there are virtually none. The reason for this is that from earliest times a village had to have a supply of water which was lacking on the Downs. It is, therefore, a wonder to find a village here in the first place, but in the past, in the winter, there was a constant flow of water down the side of the road from Crawley Pond to Kings Somborne. When the springs rose in February and March, the road became completely flooded, and at the beginning of the century the journey between the two villages was once made by boat. Thus, water from Crawley always drained into the Test Valley, but if a regular supply of water was required, the Village was dependent on excavated domestic wells.

Crawley, once known as Crow Valley, or Crawanlea - the 'glade of the crows' - does not appear to have had any natural advantages, except its sheltered position in a fold of the Downs. Nevertheless, there has been a community living here for over 1,000 years, and two books have been written about it. The first of these *Crawley - Glimpses into the Past of a Hampshire Parish* was privately published in 1907 by F W Pledge M.A., originally tutor to young George Philippi of Crawley Court. It records the first mention of Crawley in an Ecclesiastical Deed of 909 and takes its history through to the mid-nineteenth century. We wish now that he had brought it right up to the time in which he was writing, because, during all the period of which he has written, nothing remarkable happened. In 1927, a second book was published by an American couple, Mr. and Mrs. N S B Gras, *The Economic and Social History of an English Village, Crawley, Hampshire, 909-1928* (Harvard University Press 1930). This is an excellent book of its kind, well annotated with a bibliography and of great value, no doubt, to a student of rural affairs. It does, however, bring us briefly up to the date in which it was completed, i.e. 1927, and tells us a little about the arrival of the great Otto Ernst Philippi (always known as Ernest Philippi). Here again, it confirms that for a thousand years nothing of historical interest ever happened; though it does record that, in 1927, 43 households each had a bicycle, 16 a radio and 13 each had a car.

The Church of Crawley, Hampshire (13th century)

St. Mary 's Church, Crawley by Jack Northeast

Crawley was originally Church land and the 'living' was such that in the Middle Ages and beyond it always supported the appointment of a Rector who occupied his time in more important church affairs. He did not reside there but left a Curate to minister to this parish and the parish of Hunton, three or four miles away across the Downs. The Rectors were distinguished and learned men, and to one of them we owe the basic restoration of the church to its present state in the 1890s. Nevertheless, nothing much happened at Crawley, although the Prince Regent at one time leased Rookley Manor, which is situated within the Parish and from where he hunted. A real tennis court was also built at Crawley Court - it is said for his entertainment - but this was burnt down during the Second World War.

Crawley Court was the big house of the Village and was originally sited just behind the present church. In the nineteenth century, it gradually fell into a state of decay, having been occupied by the Meyer family from around the turn of the eighteenth century. Their wealth came from the sugar trade of the West Indies, which declined following the abolition of slavery in the 1830s. In 1875 a banker, Adam Kennard, bought it and completed a splendid new Victorian house to the design of the then President of RIBA[1]. He quarrelled with him before it was finished, dismissed him and finished the job under his own direction. Sadly, however, his wife died in 1880 at the age of 40. The house, estate and village gradually deteriorated, and for some considerable time was on the market. According to Mr. and Mrs. Gras, a Hampshire Guide of 1900 refers to it as the dilapidated and unattractive village of Crawley. If we look at some of the photographs taken at the beginning of the century, its unpaved road, broken fences, dilapidated barns and cottages, and vegetable gardens running down to the street can only confirm this impression.

The population - according to the census - apart from periods of plague and pestilence, has remained in the 350-500 bracket down to this day. Agriculture in the nineteenth century was far from prosperous and the Hampshire Downs were no exception, so that the inhabitants of the Village were, for the most part, extremely poor. It is not surprising that, like many other rural villagers, they departed, either attracted to the big towns by the Industrial Revolution or by emigration overseas. Fifty years ago, Pledge names three families still in the Village who could trace their residence back 300 years. Today there is no family that can go back before 1900. All the families, therefore, whose ancestors lie in the churchyard, have gone and, even in the relatively new Parish Council cemetery, there are unkempt

---

[1] Royal Institute of British Architects

graves because there are no local resident families even remotely connected with them.

The land was farmed by yeoman farmers during the eighteenth and nineteenth centuries. It was only the arrival of Ernest Philippi at the turn of the century that brought the Village into the ownership of the big house - Crawley Court. In the early 1930s the Estate and the Village properties were sold individually, bringing an influx of new residents who were mainly retired people. By the 1960s, farm mechanisation was beginning to reduce the numbers required to work on the land and, at the same time, the industrialisation of Hampshire was producing a mounting population growth until, finally, in 1969 the electrification of the London to Bournemouth Railway line turned Winchester itself into a commuting centre for Londoners. The effect has been the same for all villages on the fringe of industrial belts - they become "dormitory villages" with a constantly changing population. The price of housing rises to astonishing heights; all is change and there are no more communities with roots in the past. Crawley is now an attractive and beautiful village. Before all is forgotten, it is worth recording the initiative of a remarkable man effected the transformation and gave it a little-known link with industrial history.

J & P Coats Ltd, Advertisement Circa 1884

The Story of Ernest Philippi and J & P Coats

The story of the man who did so much to change Crawley is also part of the story of J & P Coats Ltd. (now Coats Patons Ltd), the cotton thread manufacturers, and the way in which this great enterprise was directed for a period of 15 years from Crawley.

It was at Paisley near Glasgow in the early part of the nineteenth century that two families, the Coats and the Clarkes, started to make cotton sewing thread at about the same time. By the 1840s they had built up the two most successful businesses of this kind in the world. By the 1860s they were exporting world-wide and ran up against each other, particularly in the

CSA[2], so that by the 1870s and 1880s there was intense rivalry between them. Towards the end of the century, local industry was being developed abroad and tariff barriers began to go up against them, so much so that it was appreciated that they would have to manufacture in these overseas countries. This was the golden age of the British exporter, but exports had to give way to an entirely new concept of using British capital, equipment and 'know-how' within these overseas territories. These two already successful companies could not compete in overseas markets and against each other; in 1889, an ingenious form of semi-merger was entered into. In 1890 J & P Coats Ltd became a public-quoted company with a capital of £ 5,750, 000 and with profits of £555,000. In 1896, the full merger took place with Clarkes and, shortly afterwards, with two other smaller family companies, Brooks and Chadwicks.

By 1900 J & P Coats had achieved profits of £3,000,000 and had become by far Britain's largest and most successful industrial empire earning more than the next two largest companies, Imperial Tobacco and Arthur Guinness, combined. These were fabulous figures in those days considering they were made from selling cotton thread. The fruits of the merger in 1896 were still to come. By the First World War there were 40 overseas manufacturing companies, one of the largest being in Russia where everything was lost as a result of the Revolution. In spite of the two world wars, the great Depression of the 1930s, the massive shrinkage of the British Cotton Industry and the growth of synthetic fibres, this great

---

[2] Confederate States of America, made up of the eleven, secessionist slave-holding states of the United States, existing from 1861 to 1865.

company, a household name throughout the world, still survives and flourishes.

The name of Ernest Philippi is remembered today at Coats as the greatest commercial genius of his day and the man who, in his forty years with the company, took over the direction of a large and successful business and developed it beyond anyone's imagination at the time. In doing so, he made himself a fortune and transformed a small Hampshire village, where he is buried. This village is perhaps his only memorial, as will be seen. He was born at Solingen in Prussia in 1847 of a Hamburg banking family of Greek descent. In early life, he did not enjoy good health and his first efforts to establish himself in business were not successful. He tried his luck in New York, but returned home to Germany and worked for Wulf & Co in Hamburg, who were Coats' agents in the late 1870s. He was invited by Coats to make a sales trip for them to South America, Mr. Wulf himself having been invited in the first place to make the trip. He made a most successful trip with the result that, at the age of 30, he was offered by Coats, and accepted, the job of being responsible for all overseas sales, other than the USA and Europe, and the latter territory he soon took over. Within two years he had gained the complete confidence of the Coats family and became their Chief Executive. That one of the most successful family businesses should select a young German - although he was a naturalized British subject - shows remarkable judgment on their part; but they had selected a remarkable man. What is more, they continued to work in the business themselves.

It was Ernest Philippi who, early in 1888, brought forward his ideas to harmonise the prices of three or four thread firms - not by amalgamation, but by forming a simple organisation for selling the wares of the Group as a whole and independent of production. It was called the Central Selling Organisation and was to operate throughout the world. Philippi made it work and to do so he must have, in turn, gained the confidence of Clarkes, Brookes and Chadwicks, the other firms who came into the scheme. This concept of retaining their business but joining the Central Selling Organisation was a vital stage in the final amalgamation, which took place in 1896. It made no difference to the continued efficient operation of the Central Selling Organisation, which remained in being after the amalgamation and still under the control of Philippi. This organisation was in itself his most important contribution to the development of the firm and was the result of years of frustrated efforts to achieve such a result by more traditional methods. It was brought about by determination, a brilliant mind and a facility, backed by logic, for persuading others to accept his ideas. Mr. Lever, later Lord Leverhulme[3], publicly acknowledged his debt to Philippi in his subsequent organisation of the soap industry on similar lines in what was later to become Unilever Ltd.

Ernest Philippi had already established tight overseas financial control and, far in advance of his time, developed a system of budgeting for sales demand on a worldwide basis, from which he had all the necessary statistics despatched regularly to Glasgow. He had outstanding financial ability, a fabulous memory for facts, was multilingual and a born organiser, allied to a personality that inspired confidence. He was convinced of the almost limitless expansion possibilities for sewing thread. He watched the World

[3] Industrialist, philanthropist and politician, William Hesketh Lever, First Viscount Leverhulme (1851-1925) established Lever Brothers in 1896, one of the first companies to manufacture soap from vegetable oils.

Population grow by 10,000,000 a year and he saw the sensational spread of the sewing machine - (Singers in 1880 sold 538,000 machines). As he expanded Coats' influence throughout the world, he either acquired an interest in an existing company abroad, or he built new factories. Cotton was a volatile commodity; somewhere along the line you expect to read of some disaster or error of judgment; but if there was one, it was not recorded.

Coats, as a result, made a great deal of money. Philippi, starting with a salary of £500 per annum and a quarter percent commission on certain sales, was before long earning a huge annual income and was on the way to making his fortune. His whole life was devoted to the interests of the firm, and he insisted on efficiency and integrity. Rigid in his own high standards of business morality, he expected others to accept these same standards. He exercised absolute control over personnel, and, as he appointed overseas executives, he gave them exact travel instructions and expected them to be adhered to. Summoning one man (later to assume head of Coats in Italy), he said: "You are going abroad for several months to learn German." "Very good," was the reply. "We'll make the arrangements at once." "Who's we?" replied Ernest Philippi. "My wife," said the young man. "But your wife's not going," came the last word. "I'm not going to have you sitting at night with your wife learning to talk bad German."

Philippi was understandably autocratic and intolerant of opposition, but would listen to reasoned arguments and drove both himself and his staff hard. So much so that, at the age of 53, at the turn of the century, his doctor strongly advised him to retire (which he could well afford to do) and live in a kinder climate than Glasgow. He accordingly handed in his resignation which, with Coats at the peak of its prosperity, dismayed the Board. In resigning he announced that he had found and purchased an estate at Crawley in Hampshire, and that was where he intended to live. He was told that they could not possibly afford to lose him, and that if he could attend the monthly Board meetings in Glasgow, he could continue to run the business from Crawley. He was also pressed on the grounds of personal friendship and was finally persuaded to withdraw his resignation and to continue to direct the great empire from a country village, four and a half miles from Winchester. To everyone, this must have appeared an extraordinary arrangement, especially as he abhorred the telephone and refused to have one installed in his house. Communication was by letter and a stream of telegrams, a boy being employed full time to deliver and fetch telegrams from the Village Post Office.

Crawley Court from the South by Jack Northeast

His move to Crawley in 1901 was regarded by some as a form of semi-retirement, and the disappearance from the Glasgow scene of Mr. Philippi, as he was always known by everyone, must have been a notable event. Nevertheless, it appears that his control of the business remained absolute. All the sales, production and financial figures now went through Crawley. He still wrote the Chairman's annual speech and insisted on building up a position of immense financial strength. We know that there

The Dining Room at Crawley Court by Jack Northeast

was a stream of overseas visitors, of whom at least one arrived ill-equipped for the size and status of his host's liveried establishment. His wife remained in her room for two days until suitable clothes had been purchased and brought down from London for her to appear in. On another occasion, we find two Spanish businessmen, brought over at Philippi's instigation in order to agree an amalgamation, being locked in a room together until they had come to their senses. The visitors' book for those years would make interesting reading. Like many a successful businessman since, and with the example of the magnificent land establishments of his fellow Coats directors before him, he must have looked forward to becoming a country squire and to re-vitalising the rundown estate which he had purchased. He is described at the time as being a stocky and massive man with a big square head, round face and sharp eyes, peering through thick glasses - his eyesight having been damaged early in life by typhoid fever. His family (then) consisted of his wife Magda, two sons Alex and George, and two daughters Dora and Kate (who died in her teens - a great sadness to him). As a family man, he was said to be kind and considerate and, whenever he was away, he wrote to his wife every day. He was a man of the highest moral principles but, curiously enough, not a churchman. He gave generously to charity and was undoubtedly also generous in a paternalistic way to the villagers of Crawley. Everyone appears to have been frightened of him.

A Philippi family group taken in the mid 1890 with (centre) Ernest and Magda Philippi and younger son, George. Elder son Alex is second from the left, and on the right daughters Dora and Kate.

The Reconstruction of Crawley

Ernest Philippi was living at Largs near Glasgow with a sizeable establishment, and this he was to move lock stock and barrel to Crawley. Various members of his staff, cattle and even loads of local Scottish gravel (to be laid round the new house) were included in the move. The Estate which he had bought was situated in a nondescript village, four and a half miles from Winchester, and off the beaten track on the Hampshire Downs, which were then primarily used for rearing sheep. Crawley Court, although comparatively modern, had been badly neglected and the Estate had been on the market for some time. Its real potential was development as a sporting estate. The Court did not at that time own the village cottages. There is in existence an interesting record of what the Village looked like before Philippi re-built it and again, in his son's time, at the end of the 1920s. It must indeed have been a sorry looking place. The thatched cottages had old brick, or even dirt floors, with outside sanitation and water from a few communal wells. The dirt road was unpaved with no side walk. Mr. and Mrs. Gras, writing in 1927, only 10 years after his death, tell us that, soon after Philippi's arrival, he let it be known that he would pay good prices for cottages. Presently they were being offered for sale, in some cases the stipulation being that the Vendors should remain as tenants for their lifetime. By 1908 most of the cottages and houses had been bought.

Thus, the scene was set for the creation of a model village concept which, with all his experience of industrial communities, must have come as a natural consequence of acquiring a run-down estate which required capital to revive it. According to Mr. and Mrs. Gras, Philippi was more of a builder than an agriculturalist, and he would order carts to go off on some construction enterprises when they were needed in the fields. Thus, he proceeded on an extraordinary programme of new building, often using old materials from demolished properties - modernising and reconstructing. To do this he built up an Estate building team consisting of: five carpenters: Messrs. Riggs, Thick, Cochrane, Short, and Douglas, two bricklayers and two painters, all under Mr. Broadway, the Estate Building Foreman. An architect, a Mr. Fryers, a frequent visitor to the Court, was employed. Models were made of the new Fox and Hounds Inn and the Old Rectory (renamed the Dower House) from which the builders worked. These models survived until the Estate was sold in the early 1930s when they were broken up. They illustrate how the work of reconstruction was carried out - undoubtedly under Philippi's very personal direction. Once, as he made his rounds, an estate carpenter addressed a remark to him and was told never to speak before being spoken to as he had succeeded in interrupting his train of thought. He was also quick to detect any litter and have it removed.

In 1900, there were two public houses - the Fox and Hounds run by a Mr. Francis (universally known as Monkey Brand, a popular soap at that time) - the inn being confined to the half of the building nearest the Pond and the second being the Jolly Sportsman which had stables - undoubtedly used for the main activity in these parts which was racing and the training of racehorses on the Downs. Neighbouring Stockbridge before the First World War was a great racing centre with a large number of public houses, most of which had stables attached, and a racecourse of which only the ruins of the grandstand remain. On race days, the excitement was widespread.

THE FOX AND HOUNDS before and after reconstruction

The Village Street and Hall before 1914 and the same scene today

ORCHARD COTTAGES before and after reconstruction

One local resident can still remember, as a boy, going to the nearby Rack and Manger public house on the Stockbridge-Winchester road and seeing a German band and a dancing bear on their way to the Races. In Crawley, at one time, Lord Folkestone had rented a house to run his own racing stables. The Jolly Sportsman was finally closed down when Ernest Philippi had acquired it and the reconstruction of the present Fox and Hounds had been completed. He saw no necessity for two public houses. The only evidence of The Jolly Sportsman's previous existence are the rings for tying up horses on the wall of the Homestead, a house just opposite the Village Hall.

Horse Ties

There already existed a post office, a blacksmith's forge, a small bakery and a cobbler's. The blacksmith's forge was moved; there was a new bakery; a laundry and a fine new fire house was built at the Pond - for fire had featured frequently in the history of Crawley. Perhaps one of the most important developments was the setting up of a village shop, selling at wholesale prices and subsidized by Ernest Philippi, and the erection of a really splendid village hall together with a covered roller-skating rink (burnt down in 1930) which enclosed on three sides a bowls lawn. The Village Hall became the centre of communal activity and was known as the Club. Roller skates were provided for those using the new rink, and ice skates were available for skating on the Pond when conditions permitted. There were three boats for use in summer on the Pond. A band was started, instruments provided, and a bandmaster from Winchester came out once a week to train it. The bowling green was popular and cricket was played under the name of Crawley Court Cricket Club. The Football Club played with shirts on which the badge was a black crow on a yellow background. While the work of housing improvements went on, the community of Crawley was, therefore, exceptionally well catered for at Philippi's expense.

There were new houses built adjacent to the Fox and Hounds to replace a derelict ruin and further up the village Oak Cottages, a pseudo Tudor building divided into three residences, was to follow the style of the Fox and Hounds facade. Today, nearly seventy years later, weathering is already deceiving visitors as to their genuine period character. There was also a remarkable facelift for Orchard Cottages just above the Fox and Hounds on the opposite side. It was given the appearance of a Bavarian villa and the top floor became a single room available as a dormitory for male Estate staff. Apart from the removal of an outside ladder leading up to the balcony, its outside remains unchanged today, although it is now divided into two residences.

Crawley Court required substantial renovation before Ernest Philippi moved there in August 1901. He also maintained a London house, and one of his household staff, who is still alive today, remembers going up with the other members of his domestic staff to run the house when he was there. They went to Winchester station by wagonette, which made regular trips each way to Winchester for other members of the staff. In 1911, he acquired the Rectory (having built a new Rectory in exchange) and was to lavish a great deal of attention on this. Substantial additions were made, including the square which contained a water tank and the entrance gate carried the village symbol of a crow. It was re-named the Dower House and was fitted out with panelling and antique furniture. It was finally occupied by Ernest Philippi's daughter, Dora, who died there in 1924. Dora, who lived at the Court, also took a regular part in the life of the Village. She ran sewing and dressmaking classes and a cookery class for the girls in the kitchen at Orchard Cottages where there was a cook to look after the male lodgers.

The whole appearance of the main street was improved when his gardeners were made responsible for the planting out of the cottage gardens facing the street. This was an extraordinary idea but rather more presentable than vegetable gardens which were now to be located to the rear of the cottages.

With the reconstruction and modernisation of almost the entire Village, water supply still remained a problem. There was one common domestic well opposite the village shop, and each of the large houses had their own well, but in drought years the level of the domestic wells also fell to a low level. Today we have little idea of the importance of the Village Pond to an agricultural community. From it, water was carted to the livestock in the fields and, if the Pond went dry, it was necessary to go to Stockbridge to bring water for the cattle. In the Parish Council minutes, dating from 1894 down to the present day, there has been one recurring theme - the Pond.

By 1906 Philippi was sharing the cost of £100 to repair the Pond and prevent it leaking. Again, at Philippi's instigation in 1907, a scheme and an estimate for improving the storage capacity of the Pond, at a cost of no less than £350, was proposed. The expenditure of the large sum was opposed. The matter was only carried at a village meeting by 43-12 after

Philippi had pointed out that a sufficient supply of water for agricultural machines, road engines, horses, cattle and sheep was required for the work on which the majority of the electors was employed. A small pumping engine was then installed by the Pond for filling up the water wagons but, today, the only reminder of the Pond's former importance is the metal horse trough which now has few customers! In 1929 his son, George Philippi finally solved the water problem by having it piped out to Crawley by the Southampton Water Company. Gas was brought out at the same time; the Village Street was lit up by gas standards, and the Parish Council duly appointed a lamp lighter. Some of these standards can still be seen in the Village Street.

Insurance Company Insignia and Gas Bracket on Pear Tree Cottage

The programme of reconstruction was interrupted by the First World War. Ernest Philippi's two sons both served in the British Army, but, as the war progressed, every German and anything to do with Germany became intensely unpopular. Life clearly became extremely difficult for Ernest Philippi and, no doubt, for those German members of the Coats staff who had been with them for many years. He had set up a small hospital at his own expense for wounded British soldiers; nevertheless, there were innuendoes and implications as to his loyalty and, on 22 May, 1915, he issued a statement in *The Hampshire Chronicle* as follows:

There is no doubt in my mind that the responsibility for the war rests on Germany, and that for many years past she planned it and prepared for it. Whilst hoping that Great Britain would hold aloof for at least a time, the destruction of British sea power was the real objective of a war deliberately forced upon France and Russia when the time was thought propitious. Certain methods of warfare to which Germany has resorted are so inhuman and wicked that they disgrace those who are responsible for them. Those with whom I am personally acquainted know that I have all along held and expressed these views. My two sons are both in the Army. 1 was born in Prussia, but came to this country before I was of age. Forty-eight years ago, I was, at my request, released from my allegiance as a Prussian subject. Five years later I became a naturalized British subject. I have submitted to Major St. A B Warde, the Chief Constable of Hampshire, my certificate of naturalization and a document issued by the Prussian Ministry of the Interior on 8 March 1867, to the effect that I had ceased on that day to be a Prussian subject.

In the summer of 1916 he finally retired from J & P Coats, and shortly afterwards, at the end of January 1917, his wife died. This was a blow from which he never recovered, for he died in his sleep less than three weeks later, on 10 February, 1917, at the age of 70. There was no obituary published in the *Hampshire Chronicle* - just the bare notice of his death. The Parish Council minutes only record his replacement as a member following his decease.

His elder son, Alex, who was some years older than his brother, had become a Director of J. & P. Coats in 1908, charged with maintaining liaison with Overseas Directors and Management. When his father died, he would have nothing to do with the Estate and took his share of his father's fortune in other forms. Thus, it was that his brother, George

Philippi, who was born in 1890, succeeded to the Estate and, after the First World War, enthusiastically took up where his father had left off.

George had apparently been most reluctant to leave the family home in Scotland where he was born, and was only consoled when he was promised that his boat would be brought down in the move. He used it on Crawley Pond; when the springs were up, he took it down, on occasions, on the flooded road to Kings Somborne, finally achieving a journey from Crawley to Kings Somborne in it. The boat was subsequently kept in the real tennis court and was destroyed by the fire which burnt it down in the Second World War.

Portrait of Lt. Col. George Philippi M.C. by Sir William Orpen[4]

His children eyed it from time to time, hoping that conditions would one day permit the feat to be repeated. They never did. When he arrived at Crawley Court, George was not sent away to school as he had a weak constitution and, in any case, was his father's favourite. Ernest Philippi

---

[4] The Irish-born Sir William Orpen (1878-1931) was a well-known society portrait painter, better remembered today for his documentation of trench warfare and the battles of the First World War.

preferred to have him at home under a tutor. Thus, Mr. F W Pledge was engaged as tutor and subsequently married Clara, a relative of Mrs. Philippi. When George went to Oxford University in 1908, Mr. Pledge started a Crammers for University Entrance Exams at Crawley Manor and ran a popular establishment there for twenty years. Ernest Philippi must have helped the couple by making a substantial addition to the size of the Manor, which he let to them probably at a modest rent to accommodate sufficient pupils. These were made welcome to the sporting facilities of the Court, and at least two former pupils recall having had a marvellous time at Crawley. Pledge's success as a crammer was due to a thorough knowledge of all the likely examination questions and the regularity of their re-appearance.

George kept fairly regular diaries from 1904 up until the First World War. From them we are able to obtain a picture of the Philippi family at Crawley Court which was frequently full of visitors. He often notes that he is accompanying Papa to inspect the Dower House, take a walk around the Village, and that every now and then Papa is in a rage about something but has calmed down later in the day. He worked with his tutor, Mr. Pledge, every day but had plenty of time for sporting activities. At the age of 14 he was an ardent golfer and no doubt, under the guidance of Douglas, the Head Gardener, who had moved South to Crawley with his father, laid out the little golf course adjacent to the Court on the West side. Douglas was a good golfer, and on summer evenings George and he often played with Pledge and Robertson the Estate Manager. He also travelled by car regularly to Bramshott and other courses to play in competitions and faithfully recorded all his scores. Apart from his lifetime interest in shooting, hunting and riding, he was an exceptionally keen billiards player, which probably accounts for the three billiard tables still in use in the Village Hall today. We read of the increasing use of motor cars - a Panhard, a Mercedes, a Hispano and a de Deitrich were all mentioned. On 30 September, 1913, there is an entry "pottered about with the tractor which came yesterday" - which tells us that his father had, as might be expected, taken an early interest in farm mechanisation.

Although George's elder brother, Alex, was at home frequently, it was George for whom all the sporting activities of the Estate were created in the first place, for his father certainly never used them. His interest lay in looking after the village he was re-creating, in the welfare of those who worked for him and the farming activities. Perhaps it was not so surprising that Alex, who had a useful function to perform as a Director of J & P Coats, should not choose to inherit the Estate. His younger brother had, however, been brought up in its tradition and had no training whatever for a commercial occupation.

With the outbreak of the First World War George joined the Royals - a Cavalry Regiment - but, following an illness which laid him up for some months, managed to transfer to the Royal Flying Corps where there was a certain prospect of seeing action. He was in 60 Squadron and won the Military Cross for shooting down enemy observation balloons, but was ultimately shot down himself and wounded, and ended the war on Lord Trenchard's staff. (Lord Trenchard has always been credited with the foundation of the RAF as an independent force). After the War, his flying connections sometimes brought visitors to Crawley who landed their light aeroplanes adjacent to Crawley Court, and in the Second World War George Philippi became a Commander in the RAF.

When George Philippi inherited the Estate, Oak Cottages, the pseudo Tudor cottages halfway up the Village street, on the left-hand side, had not been completed and were then finished. George added a communal bath house adjacent to Pond House, opposite the Fire House. This contained four baths - the ladies bathing on Tuesday night, the men on Friday. Soap was provided and you brought your own towel. The Bath House became a garage in the early 1930s, but the graffiti still serves as a reminder of its former use.

During the 1920s Crawley Court was at the height of its fame as a country estate with every sporting activity. The shoot was improved by spending money and planting judicious belts of trees and shrubs to give the best result for holding game. When the sale of the Estate took place in June 1932, the game bag for the previous year was given in the particulars of sale as follows: pheasants 4,702, partridge 913, hare 587, rabbits 14,104, various 336, total 20,641, and it was recorded that a great deal of money had been spent on improving the shoot. There was the golf course, tennis courts, a squash court, and a real tennis court - the cricket ground which used to be adjacent to the Court having been removed to its present site at the top of Hacks Lane.

Farming operations had been extended. During the war, as a contribution to the production of food, much of the Estate was ploughed up with results which were later to prove disastrous. In 1922, a Professor Wibberly, an Irish agriculturalist and grassland expert, was engaged as Farm Manager and came to live at Pond House, which not only had the Bath House added but also a farm office; the stone steps are still in the outside wall so that the office might be approached without going through the house. He brought in entirely novel ideas. He even developed a marrow kale - *Brassica Wibberlii* - and there was a pedigree flock of sheep. The whole Wibberly enterprise was reviewed in an article in *Country Life* in September 1926. In a paper which Professor Wibberly published in 1928 entitled *Present Agricultural Methods* which he used at Crawley, he states that he was successful from 1922-25, but from 1926-28 he was faced with 'uncontrollable difficulties'. Sad to relate the theories never bore fruit and the losses, by 1928, had reached the staggering sum of £18,000[5] in a year, which was a considerable sum of money in those days. The farming losses coincided with The Great Wall Street Crash of 1929 and the depression in world stock markets which followed. Each took its toll of George Philippi's fortune and the Crawley Court estate became an intolerable burden. We find that it was let for three months in the summer of 1930 to Nubar Gulbenkian[6] who, in his biography *Pantaraxia*[7], gives a pleasant description of the enjoyable time he spent there and the facilities that it offered.

The impending doom of the Estate must have cast a shadow over the community. On 5 May, 1931, the main part of the Village was put up for sale, including the Dower House, the White House, and the Fox and Hounds. It was followed just over a year later, 14 June, 1932, with the main Estate which was described as "one of the most noted freehold residential and sporting estates in the County." There could have been no worse time

---

[5] In today's money £1,036,800.
[6] Nubar Gulbenkian (1896-1972) was an Armenian business magnate and renowned socialite, to whom the following quote is attributed: "I've had good wives; as good wives go, two of them went."
[7] An expression coined by Gulbenkian, meaning any action aimed at keeping people on their toes.

for selling land and property, and the prices realised in both sales look ludicrous by today's standards. It was the depth of the Depression.

By arrangement with the purchaser of the Estate, George Philippi continued to lease Crawley Court and to live there until his death in 1953.

The Changing Face of Crawley

Crawley was in no way a beautiful village at the turn of the century. If there had been a Planning Authority at this time, the reconstruction of the Village would probably never have been carried out - certainly not with the speed with which it was undertaken. There could have been no quarrel with the major tidying up operations such as pulling down old barns, clearing away cottages which had literally fallen down, and introducing a Tudor style with an adjacent dash of Bavaria thrown in. We find Mr. and Mrs. Gras, writing in 1927, just ten years after Ernest Philippi had died, as follows:

He gave Crawley the appearance of a model village almost devoid of a single striking corner or nook, which is neat and seems clean, but none of it is the object of an artist's pilgrimage.

It pre-supposes that inevitable effect of the impact of industrial capital on rural life, but Crawley had become a finer village in which to live. We know that George Philippi had completed his father's work and, in 1927, Mr. and Mrs. Gras were obviously not impressed with its appearance. What has happened in the meantime to transform the situation is the growth of the trees and the shrubs throughout the village, which has had a remarkable softening effect on the general outline. In a post-World War Two development on the hill at the South of the Village, a few modern houses were put up and even these have now been absorbed in the landscape by the trees and shrubs which have been planted around them.

All the credit cannot be given to the trees and shrubs because there is many an erstwhile attractive Hampshire village which is bedecked by petrol filling station signs and advertisements, a tin roof or two and the inevitable 'infilling'. Crawley today is still a parish of around 500 people and its only commercial activity is now one public house. We owe that state of affairs to remarkable foresight. George Philippi, at the time of the sale of the Village, vested in Crawley Court an important restrictive covenant on future development which was to prove vitally protective in the period immediately following the Second World War. Restrictive covenants are included in the sale of many properties giving them protection against loss of light and other amenities, but many of them are never enforced for lack of action on behalf of the holder of the covenant. There was one man in Crawley, Lt. Col. J Whitney, a retired regular soldier who lived at Little Thatch, and it was he who successfully organised the owner residents in the upholding of these restrictive covenants. Efforts to start a garage, tea gardens, etc., were frustrated and, finally, it was necessary for the Owner Residents to organise themselves and seek the assistance of the law in preventing the Dower House and its surrounding land from becoming a pig farm. The winning of this case enabled any threat of undesirable development, including the exhibition of advertisements and so on, to be frustrated. The Planning Authority designated it an "area of outstanding natural beauty" and a Tree Preservation Order was obtained. However irksome Col. Whitney's tireless activity may have been at the time, his name must be coupled with that of the Philippis in presenting today's pleasant scene. In the meantime, a few years ago, the post office facilities were withdrawn and the village shop finally closed. In some ways, the first closure precipitated the second. People had to go to Winchester to draw their pensions and inevitably used the big multiple stores with their lower prices. Thus, the last commercial activity, apart from The Fox and Hounds, has gone.

Crawley Court has also disappeared. In 1970 the Bon Secours Nursing Order of Nuns, who ran a nursing home there, left; the Court and its thirty-two surrounding acres were put up for sale. The Independent Broadcasting Authority bought it and, with a speed which Ernest Philippi might have appreciated, obtained planning permission to pull it down, erect a modern office block and move from London. "The Queen of Hampshire villages," as the IBA themselves described it, was to be protected from the anticipated increase in traffic. The approach road was widened and a special junction constructed on the Winchester-Stockbridge main road. Unfortunately, this also opened up an attractive short cut for through traffic. The covenant which once protected the Village has also gone. On the site, from where the threads which hold the world together were once controlled, another kind of empire reigns.

Appendix

Ernst Philippi: An Immigrant's Story

From Soligen Schoolboy to Director General of a World-Wide Sewing Cotton Combine

By Franz Hendrichs

Ernst Philippi, who was born in Solingen on 4 June 1846, had no easy time in his youth. His father, who was headmaster of the local high school, ruled both sternly at home and in school, and the seven years spent under his tuition were indeed laborious for the son, but they led to the foundations for his excellent knowledge of foreign languages.

In 1863 Ernst Philippi began his business career as a junior clerk in a Dusseldorf bank. Almost all his time was spent on inferior duties, which increased his desire for greater freedom and activity in the commercial field. From all accounts England appeared to him to be the ideal country in which to realise his aims. Accordingly, in 1867, we find him in Liverpool, established as a cotton broker on a modest scale. Failure of a large foreign deal, however, compelled him to abandon this branch of business and to return to Germany.

In Hamburg he took a post as English correspondent in a small import-export business with office premises in a basement. Amongst other business the firm acted as agents for J & P Coats of Paisley, Scotland, for the import of sewing cotton, and Philippi was responsible for the correspondence conducted with them. As typewriters were unknown in those days he had to write the letters himself, and this he did with the clear handwriting and the minute care characteristic of his person. Not only did he write in good English, but he never rested until he could submit a perfectly written letter without the slightest correction to his chief for his signature, even if it involved copying the letter several times.

And then one day the unexpected happened. The senior partner of J & P Coats appeared in the office, holding a letter in his hand and without much ado demanded to speak to the author. Self-assured, the head of the firm replied it was his letter, whereupon Coats intimated that he wished to become acquainted with the man who actually wrote the letter and the signatory. Thus compelled, the head of the firm called Philippi, who was standing at his desk in the adjoining room, agreed to converse with him alone. The conversation was typically brief, somewhat as follows:

Coats: Did you write this letter?

Philippi: Yes

Coats: Then you are appointed to my firm. I'll arrange things your chief.
        You must come to Paisley at once and get to know the business
        Then I have a job for you in Greece.

A few days later Philippi was in Scotland. He was able to carry out the transaction
in Greece to the satisfaction of the firm and thereupon Coats entrusted him with
a further task in the Argentine, which he also completed satisfactorily.

Upon his return to Paisley he had further opportunity of obtaining an insight into
the possibilities of marketing sewing cotton. Paisley – at that time a town of
50,000 inhabitants, and hour's train journey west of Glasgow and situated in a
broad valley through which the river Cart flows idly – was already dominated in
those days by two big sewing cotton firms. On the western side of the town was
the firm of J & P Coats, whose trademark was the endless chain, to the east lay
Clark & Co. with the famous anchor trademark. The latter firm was the older and
bigger undertaking of the tow. Together they employed many thousands of
women and girls, and competition between them was severe.

Then one day, after exhaustive consideration, Philippi approached Coats with the
intimation that he now had a task for him. Hitherto, he said the firm had
manufactured 3-cord, 4-cord, 5-cord, 6-cord and other types of thread as occasion
arose, thus necessitating frequent readjustment of machinery which was
detrimental to the economic conduct of the enterprise. Philippi was of the
opinion that it should be possible to determine which type of thread was most
suitable for sewing and the same time most economical from the manufacturer's
standpoint. Once this had been ascertained the manufacturing programmes
should be simplified (today we would talk of 'standardisation') and the standard
thread produced with the same number of machines as before, but far greater
quantities and at a lower price.

Astounded though he was, Coats had every inclination to follow up these
suggestions, after twenty-four hours for reflection. In fact, he forthwith instructed
Philippi to carry out his own proposal, thus setting him an immense task.
Following comparative tests in all directions, the 6-cord thread was ascertained to
be the best and, at the same time, the most economical, and the entire factory was
re-organised for the production of this standard sewing cotton. Production
increased considerably and the further problem of marketing the output now
arose.

Thenceforth Philippi travelled untiringly, in Spain, Portugal, Italy and the Balkans,
or overseas, in search of new markets for his cotton. In some countries, he had
large quantities of tiny sample reels distributed free by costumed groups to
women and girls leaving church. In others, he tried to drive his competitors from

the field by undercutting. Success was not wanting. In fact, it transcended the firm itself, for the accentuated competition induced Clark & Co to negotiate a proposal for joint action in the future. In the preliminary agreement, for which he was largely responsible on behalf of Coats, both parties agreed that the combined leadership of the two firms be assigned to the one with the largest turnover in a given period. Clark & Co relied upon their bigger works and their undoubted superiority in former years. They were, therefore, not a little surprised when the comparative figures on the appointed date revealed a considerably larger turnover for Coats and thus placed the joint management of both firms in the hands of the latter. Philippi now became Managing Director of both undertakings and during the next few years utilised the powerful position thus acquired to establish closer contact with sewing cotton firms in Great Britain and other countries. In addition, large new factories were erected in many countries, employing thousands of hands, until at last the enterprise commanded world-wide interests.

The parent factories in Paisley also underwent constant expansion. Gigantic six-storeyed brick buildings arose with broad, well-lighted work rooms, each devoted to a single process. In one the cotton fibre was carded; in the next a thin thread was spun; in the third six such strands were spun together to form the finished cotton. Finally, it was wound on wooden reels, labelled and packed for despatch, ready for consignment. In addition to these extensive part-factories there were a number of subsidiary works, in particular the dye works and the premises for the manufacture of the reels. Shiploads of timber, already square-cut were constantly on the way from Canada to Scotland. Adjoining the timber piles were long workshops on both sides of which automatic drilling machines and turning lathes were set up. Each machine turned out about a hundred finished reels per minute. The wood shavings were ejected on to a broad moving leather band, running the length of the building and were thus removed. Everything was carried out in a business-like manner, but at a pace bearing the mark of success. Although the workers in all departments were only needed for the supervision of machines, more than 20,000 persons were employed in the two factories in Paisley during the nineties, of whom only about 2000 were men.

The direction of all these undertakings at home and abroad centred in Glasgow, where Philippi had created a holding company named The Central Agency Ltd, which was accommodated in a many-storeyed, representative building, lavishly decorated with marble internally. In a large office, the incoming mail from all quarters of the globe was opened by the confidential clerks, while 300 officials of the firm were responsible for supervising and regulating the output of all the firms embraced by the concern. In the top storey, a variety of testing machines was in constant activity, testing the manufactured sewing cotton for strength, fast colour, and length spooled.

At the head of The Central Agency and of the Board was Ernst Philippi, who, although by a nature a businessman, was simultaneously chairman of the technical committees responsible for purchasing the factory equipment. In his simple but tastefully decorated office only fundamental questions were decided. At noon, he generally visited the stock exchange to discuss matters with business friends. Self-assured though he was, he was simple in manner and entirely unpretentious. To Scotchmen he was a Scotsman. He wore a beard in the Scotch styles and his pronunciation bore no trace of German. He also had an excellent mastery of French and a good knowledge of other romance languages.

At the turn of the century the capital invested in the Coats concern was equivalent to some 500 million Reichsmarks, on which a high dividend was paid for many decades. In the circumstances, it was not surprising that the former owners of Coats and Clark attained great wealth and were in a position to make many and varied endowments. The magnificent town hall, richly equipped churches, hospitals, schools, concert halls and many other buildings and public parks in and about Paisley bore witness to the fact. But all those, also, who were connected with the remarkable growth of the concern had become people of means.

Article published in *Die Heimat*, supplement to *The Solinger Tageblatt*, 25 February and 25 March, 1950. Author: Franz Hendrichs VDI (Association of German Engineers).

From *Hampshire Book Shelf*

Review by John Arlott[8]

Philippi's Crawley (from C M Printing Services, 20a Jewry Street, Winchester, £1) by I T Henderson is a history of that village – four and a half miles from Winchester – largely in relation to Otto Ernst Philippi, the man who, by 1900, had built the Glasgow firm of J & P Coats (now Coats Patons) into Britain's largest industrial concern. In that year he announced his retirement, bought Crawley Court, a Victorian building which, like the rest of the village, had become almost derelict, and announced his intention to settle there. His fellow directors held his business ability in such respect that they persuaded him to continue to control the company – even from Crawley. He consented to do so: but would go to Glasgow only for the monthly board meetings; and, since he would not have a telephone in the house, he managed the firm by letter and telegram. Indeed, his directions were so constant that one boy had to be employed full time at the village Post Office to maintain the two-way flow. He also found time to reshape Crawley. Born in Prussia, he was a stern, if basically benevolent, despot. He set out to buy most of the houses and cottages in the village, hoping, and often stipulating, that the occupiers who sold to him would continue to live in them for the rest of their lives. So he succeeded in turning the formerly dilapidated into a 'model village' – though one which was described as 'the appearance of a model village almost devoid of a single striking corner or nook, which is neat and seems clean, but none of it is the object of an artist's pilgrimage.' After his death in 1917 his son vested a restricted covenant in the estate s that subsequent residents in the village were able to resist commercial 'development' until, in 1970, the Independent Broadcasting Authority bought the manor, demolished it, built a modern office block on the site and moved into what they described as 'the Queen of Hampshire Villages'.

Published in *Hampshire, The County Magazine*, September 1977, Vol.17, No. 11.

---

[8] The Hampshire born, John Arlott (1914-1991) was a journalist, author, poet, cricket broadcaster and the incomparable voice of the BBC's Test Match Special.

www.ingramcontent.com/pod-product-compliance
Lightning Source LLC
Chambersburg PA
CBHW050950030426
42339CB00007B/365